For my children, nieces, nephews, and all the kids of the world who will combat this pending crisis. — D.H.

First edition

Text and Illustrations copyright © 2021 by Verdani Institute for the Built Environment

All rights reserved. No part of this book may be reproduced in any manner with the express written consent of Verdani Institute for the Built Environment, except in the case of brief excerpts in critical reviews or articles. All inquiries should be addressed to info@verdani-institute.org.

Visit our website at www. https://www.verdani-institute.org/, or visit this book's companion website at https://charity.gofundme.com/o/en/campaign/2020vibechildrensbook.

Printed by Amazon Kindle Direct Publishing

Library of Congress Control Number: 978-1-7368-6690-0

Paperback ISBN: 978-1-7368-6691-7

Text by Daniele Horton | Illustrations by Maia Batumashvili
Editing by Melissa Sherman Pearl | Book design by Ryan Hasan

Once upon a time, nearly 14 billion years ago, there was a ginormous explosion. It was packed with heat and energy and enough particles to create the universe. 10 billion years after this event that scientists named the Big Bang, our very own Earth was born.

Young Earth was beautiful. Covered in lush forests and deep oceans, she became home to millions of animal species and humans, too. With clean air and water, everyone lived in harmony with the natural environment.

Recently Earth has started to develop a fever. This slow and steady rise in Earth's temperature is called global warming and it's not good for plants, animals, or people.

It's hard to see someone you love not feeling well acknowledged a group of compassionate kids. Why was she sick? How could they help Earth feel better and strengthen the climate for all living organisms?

"If we can fix the climate, everyone will feel better and be healthier," said Isabella.

"We would need superheroes for that," Gabriel responded.

"Are you kidding?" exclaimed Lucas. "We are the superheroes! We can be Climate Heroes!"

"YEAH!!!" they all shouted together.

"We just need a little bit of help," said Gabriel.

The hopeful heroes were excited to ask their parents for help. "We love your enthusiasm but can we talk about this later?" said both Mom and Dad. Not happy to wait until the end of their parents' work day, the kids had another meeting.

"Let's figure out what we can do ourselves right now," said Gabriel.

"That sounds great!" said Isabela.

"Yes," the other kids said. "We can do this! We can save the earth!"

They rushed to the one place they knew they could find information: the library! Thanks to the books on the shelves and online research they learned about steps they could take to help the earth. They also read that carbon emissions from used energy along with heat-trapping greenhouse gases were hurting the environment. But what exactly does that mean and how did it happen in the first place?

About 150 years ago, the Industrial Revolution was in full swing. People constructed big machines to produce everything from shoes and cookware to farm tools and even bigger machines. These large factories used fossil fuels for power. When burned, these fuels send carbon emissions in the form of smoke, gases, liquids, and tiny particles into the environment. This pollution creates unhealthy air and water while the trapped gas can raise Earth's temperature.

A temperature increase of less than 2° Fahrenheit can barely be felt by humans but can cause major climate change. Arctic sea ice stays frozen at 30° but at 32° it can slowly melt leaving polar bears with fewer places to live. As ice melts, more water goes into the ocean causing water levels to go up worldwide. This can change coastlines and hurt many species of animals and plants.

Scientists have discovered that, like people, Earth needs a healthy, smoke-free lifestyle. Reducing the release of carbon emissions into the atmosphere will help with that. The use of cars and machinery that rely on natural renewable energy sources (like the sun and wind) instead of fossil fuels (such as coal and crude oil) is a great start. Solar power is the conversion of the sun's rays into electricity. Wind power can also be harnessed and used.

On the way home from the library, the kids stopped by their favorite park but something was different. There was trash everywhere! As self-appointed Climate Heroes, their first duty was clear. "Let's clean up the park!" the young friends exclaimed. Working together they picked up everything from candy wrappers to facemasks. They separated the trash from the recyclables and put them in the proper cans.

Proud of their accomplishments for the day, they realized that saving the earth was going to be a big job. Working together as a team, they needed a uniform to help complete their mission. They asked Grandma Fafinha to make them Earth's Climate Hero uniforms. She gathered up old sheets, clothes, and costumes from last Halloween. Working all day and night she repurposed the materials into amazing superhero regalia.

Equipped with research, experience, huge hearts and bold costumes, the heroes started a list of everything they needed to do to make Earth healthy again. They had tons of ideas. The list was getting so long that they realized they needed help fast! There was no time to waste! In order to save the earth, they would need to get the word out and recruit lots of Climate Heroes.

As soon as they finalized their list, they began spreading the word. While they started this mission at school, they continued sharing information with their friends at birthday parties, on the soccer fields, at band practice, and, maybe even more importantly, over the internet. Lots of other kids were interested, too. Working together they created a #EarthsClimateHeroes campaign to save the earth.

With the campaign underway, kids from all over the world were reaching out to our Climate Heroes. While most kids were simply inspired and eager to start their own projects others shared initiatives they had already been working on. It was so exciting to discover that even though everyone lived in different parts of the world, they could save the earth together!

Environmental creativity was alive and well all over the globe. Many kids started reforestation or tree-planting campaigns. This replenishing of forests helps keep air clean, provide shade, and reduce soil erosion. Other groups of kids gathered friends and family to help them clean local rivers, beaches and parks.  Special attention was also given to creating more gardens that would not only look pretty but produce healthy food.

Now that the Heroes had connected globally with kids, it was time to work locally with the adults. Lucas and Gabriel convinced their parents to install solar panels while Kaue explained to his family that rain barrels collect water to use in other parts of the yard. Isabela, Carolina, Gisele and Nyssa persuaded their principal to let them use a plot of land at school for a vegetable garden and fruit trees. What they all learned is that even if everyone does just a little bit, collectively it makes a big difference.

Famous throughout their town, the Climate Heroes were truly earning their name by teaching everyone about saving energy and water, recycling, using clean power and even eating less meat. The Mayor was so impressed with their campaign and actions that he came to the school to award them "Earth's Climate Heroes" medals. Other cities and communities joined forces and together they created a program to recognize all of the young climate heroes who were helping nurse Earth back to health.

But the truth was as much as the kids appreciated the recognition, they worked hard because in their hearts they knew it was the right thing to do. As more and more kids from around the world helped clean their local communities, Earth grew healthier and her fever went down. People, animals, and the environment returned to living in harmony with one another while protecting not only each other, but Earth, too.

And everyone lived happily, healthily and sustainably ever after! Our future generations will, too!

# Glossary

**Carbon Emissions:** *Carbon monoxide and carbon dioxide in the form of smoke, gases, liquids, and tiny particles that are released into the atmosphere.*

**Climate Change:** *A change in the weather conditions over a long period of time.*

**Erosion:** *The loss or movement of loose soil due to water and wind.*

**Fossil Fuels:** *Organic plant and animal remains buried deep underground that humans dig up and burn for energy.*

**Greenhouse Gases:** *Atmospheric gases like carbon dioxide and methane that trap the sun's heat.*

**Industrial Revolution:** *A time that began about 250 years ago when people discovered that machines and engines that burn fossil fuels could be used to manufacture things more cheaply and faster, so lots of new factories were built and lots of fossil fuels were burned.*

**Repurposing:** *Using an object for a different purpose instead of throwing it away.*

# How can you become an Earth's Climate Hero?

 Gather friends for group outdoor clean-ups at a park, beach, playground, or hiking trail. Make it fun with games, contests and music!

 Help plant trees, shrubs, and native plants that will thrive in your local climate, use less water and improve air quality.

 Create a fruit and vegetable garden at school or home. Make sure to use plants that attract natural pollinators like bees, butterflies, and hummingbirds.

 Instead of throwing away food scraps, leaves, and newspaper, make a compost bin. The waste will become a nutrient-rich garden soil.

 Don't forget to separate trash, recyclables, and compost into their proper cans. Remind the adults at home to replace light bulbs with energy-saving LED bulbs.

 Talk to your parents about maybe installing solar panels, getting an electric car, or adding rain barrels at home.

 Try switching to a more plant-based vegetarian or vegan diet. Meatless Mondays are a great start.

 Carry your own reusable straw, water bottle, and silverware (and encourage your family to do the same!) - just say no to plastic waste when going out.

Please share your most creative environmental efforts on social media!!
#EarthsClimateHeroes

Made in the USA
Middletown, DE
23 May 2021